# BORDER CROSSINGS

## Affirming Faith By Crossing Boundaries

Readings in the Gospel of Luke

Edited by
Alwyn Thomson

**CONTRIBUTORS:**
*David Bruce, David McMillan,
Gary Mason, Heather Morris,
Derek Poole, David Porter,
Priscilla Reid, Steve Stockman,
Michael Wardlow, Ethel White.*

**ECONI**

1999
1 874324 41 7
Design: Spring Graphics
Printed by: GPS Colour Graphics Ltd.

# Contents

# Foreword

We like to think of ourselves as a community that believes in the authority of the Bible. Even where the Bible is not read, its images and stories shape and define us as people, families and communities. Yet for all our Bible reading and knowledge, do we hear and obey the word, as that word itself demands?

Those who take the name of Christ do so on the assumption that faith is authenticated by commitment to the word of God. But we must acknowledge that our hearing and obedience is always partial and incomplete - we all have blind spots.

For many of us the greatest blind spot has been our failure to hear God's word to our broken community. While in principle we affirm Scripture's authority, in practice we have struggled to hear its challenge to us.

This book reflects our conviction that the Bible has profound relevance for our community. However, the cost of hearing this ever relevant word will be high for all who submit to its judgements. Yet in the darkness this word is light, in death this word is life, in despair this word is hope.

We invite you to join with us as we hear the word of God in the Gospel of Luke. May it be light, life and hope to us as we read, hear and obey.

**Derek Poole**
Development Officer
ECONI December 1998

# How to use this book

This book is designed to take you through Luke's Gospel over a period of ten weeks.

Each week has five readings drawn from two or three chapters of the Gospel. We suggest that you follow these readings from Monday to Friday of each week. Each day's reading has three key parts. The first is Luke's text. The Bible reference is given above the comment, which is the second part. The third is the suggestion for prayer or reflection which follows each comment.

There are two further elements. At the foot of each page is a reference to a longer section from the Gospel. By following these readings you will read through the whole of the Gospel in fifty days.

At the back of the book are five prayers for the five days of readings. Each focuses on one of the implications of the Gospel for Christian living in our community. Thus at the end of the ten weeks the reader will have worked through this cycle of prayers ten times.

Finally, we have included some background information on Luke's world, which will help the reader understand better some of the borders - political, religious and social - that Jesus crossed.

# Introduction to Luke's Gospel

For the next fifty days we will be reading Luke's Gospel. We know this story, don't we? The cast is very familiar - heavenly hosts and frightened shepherds, a pious Levite and a good Samaritan, a prodigal son and a compassionate father, a rich ruler and a poor beggar, Magdalene the sinner and Zacchaeus the tax-collector.

And in the midst of it all is Jesus: the baby in the manger, the boy in the Temple, the man on the cross. This Jesus is the consolation of Israel, the friend of sinners, the light for revelation. He is the rising sun whose glory illumines every chapter of the story. This Jesus is the heartbeat of Luke's Gospel.

But who is this Jesus? Is he a preacher of love, inspiring us to acts of greatness? Is he a proclaimer of personal salvation, calling us out of the world? These are common enough views. Yet they leave us with a Jesus who is strangely ephemeral - floating lightly over this world of ours. The footprints this Jesus leaves in the sand by the Sea of Galilee are not as deep as those of other people.

Perhaps a Jesus who touches his world lightly is free to speak to us in our very different world. But at what cost? For it seems that such a Jesus cannot easily speak to our 'rootedness' - our specific sense of identity, not just as human beings, but as particular men, women and communities, living in a particular place at a particular time.

Is this Jesus Luke's Jesus? Yes and No. Jesus does transcend his boundaries, Jesus is different, Jesus is unique - 'the Son of the most high' - but he is also Jesus of Nazareth, a Jewish carpenter, who lived in Palestine nearly 2,000 years ago.

Jesus came to a community with its own set of social attitudes, moral values, religious convictions and political aspirations. When Jesus challenged the people of this community to repent, to receive the Kingdom of God and to love their neighbours and enemies it was an all-encompassing challenge - calling them to a transformation that was social, moral, religious and political as well as personal.

Jesus wielded the hammer of the Kingdom to shatter the rock of his people's values. For these values were built, not on the solid foundation of God's truth as some might have claimed, but on the shifting sands of human weakness and prejudice.

It may seem strange, but the more Jesus connects to his world the more he connects to ours. For we too prefer to establish our own social attitudes, moral values, religious convictions and political aspirations, calling on God to sanction them. This challenge that Jesus brings is one we dare not ignore.

Luke's Gospel, written for Christians in first century Palestine and twentieth century Ireland, brings that challenge to successive generations. We may try to love our neighbour, but what if our neighbour is also our enemy? We may have come to faith in Christ and we may call others to faith, but what does faithful living mean?

We know this story, don't we? We know what will happen in this story. But as we read over the next fifty days, what will happen to us?

# Part 1
## THE EARLY YEARS

For Israel, it was a time of expectation. God had made a promise and God would keep that promise. In the interwoven stories of the births of John and Jesus, that promise was being fulfilled.

In a world in which the power of Caesar Augustus seemed absolute, the power of God was at work to bring salvation. So Mary, Elisabeth and Simeon sing their hymns to God the Saviour. The shepherds, trembling in the fields, hear the angelic proclamation of the birth of a saviour. Anna points those waiting for the redemption of Israel to Mary's child.

This salvation promises - or threatens - to turn the world upside down. It exalts the poor and oppressed, while pulling down those who would exalt themselves. It brings a new Kingdom with new values that challenges the power and authority of every human kingdom. It calls the excluded and despised into a new community that God will create, to share in its blessings and its service.

At the heart of the promise is the child Jesus - God's promise fulfilled, God's Kingdom come. But how will humanity respond? For now we hear hymns of praise, but already Simeon warns of sorrow and suffering to come.

# **1** WHEN GOD COMES NEAR

## day 1

### Outsiders know the truth

*Luke 1:1-4*

Of all the people we meet in this gospel Luke himself is one of the most intriguing.

A Gentile, he compiles a comprehensive account of the emergence of this new Jewish movement. Distant from the events at the heart of its rise, he draws on the eyewitness accounts of those who had been involved from the start. An outsider to the traditions of these people, still he had grasped the significance of promises fulfilled and the supernatural messengers that were the signs of God's coming near to Israel after four hundred years of silence.

Why should a despised Gentile take such an interest in events in hostile Judea? What made this possible? At some point in Luke's life the God of Israel came near to him. In hearing the story of Jesus he encountered the living God - the God of Gentile as well as Jew. Luke was the beloved enemy, the hungry who picked up the crumbs from the table.

The salvation that Luke presents is rooted in events among an ancient people, yet lived in the experience of outsiders like him. This was indeed good news - the truth of which we, as much as Theophilus, need to be certain.

### REFLECT

What does it mean for you to have received the truth of the good news as an outsider?

### Risky action required                    *Luke 1:46-55*

There was little in what happened to Mary that would normally be the cause of much rejoicing. She was pregnant and unmarried. Ahead there was only disgrace to her family and to Joseph. The future for both her and her child was as social outcasts. But then this was no ordinary woman.

Greeted as the favoured one, she was more perplexed than frightened by the angel's appearance. In the unfolding drama she retains the presence of mind to ask relevant questions of the angel and the openness to God of an obedient servant. Yet mindful of the social consequences of her obedience she departs to find seclusion with Elizabeth.

Her song of praise reveals the source of her confidence. God was her saviour and the world order was being transformed. What was being asked of her carried great risk. But this was consistent with God's renewed action in history. The old certainties of the proud, the powerful and the rich were being torn down. By God's mercy the lowly and hungry were recipients of the ancient promise.

God often requires us to act in ways that contradict convention but are never inconsistent with the divine character and purpose in the world. Are we prepared to take the risk?

**REFLECT**

What risks are you prepared to take in this society to live a life consistent with God's priorities and values?

### Forgiveness and peace are possible          *Luke 1:67-79*

It is hard not to feel a certain sympathy for poor Zechariah. There he was doing his duty in the Temple - probably the biggest day of his life - and God had to break with centuries of tradition and make contact. The dividing line between ritual and spiritual reality was crossed.

Most of us like to think that in answer to our prayers we would accept the word of Gabriel. Nine months is a long time to reflect on such a mistake.

Yet when Zechariah's silence is broken God again draws near. The Holy Spirit fills him and prophecy is heard in the land from the lips of one of Israel's religious leaders. The understanding that Zechariah reveals is steeped in the history of prophets and promises.

Mercy is at the heart of what follows. It is mercy (72) that undergirds the promise of salvation, made known by the forgiveness now on offer. Mercy is the energising source of the dawn that will lead to peace. It is mercy and not merit that saves us. That is as much the fact of Israel's tradition as it is of the new dawn.

Why then do we find it so hard to be merciful to others?

**PRAY**

Pray that God would teach us to be merciful just as he is merciful.

### Good news for the people

*Luke 2:8-20*

The shepherds certainly understood one thing as a result of all that happened that amazing night - they had to tell others about it. As a group of men used to the rough life they come across as practical hard thinking types. Scared they may have been but, unlike others in the story, they were quick to take at face value what they had been told and head to Bethlehem to check it out. Having done so, it was time to let others in on the good news.

The only problem was that the angel couldn't have picked a less reliable social class to start spreading the word. Shepherds weren't exactly trustworthy and there must have been a nervous smile or two between the parents when this band appeared at the stable entrance. Yet their directness was not lost on Mary whose response is contrasted with the amazement of others.

People would have been reluctant to take the word of these dodgy witnesses. If God had something to say about this child surely he would have used a more reliable source. Do you set social boundaries that cut you off from hearing what God is really doing in our community?

### PRAY

Pray for openness to hear the word of God when it comes from those we too easily dismiss.

## Salvation for the world                    *Luke 2:25-38*

Simeon and Anna were devout people, worshipping God with expectant hearts. Together, they personified the spiritual longing of Israel.

Anna was a permanent presence at the Temple. Her personal circumstances were full of symbolic reflections of Israel's relationship with God. Yet, in her tragedy, she had the rare honour for a woman of being called a prophet. Simeon had received an explicit personal promise. But the promise was two edged - seeing God's salvation was the precursor of his own death.

The Holy Spirit brought these two - children of the promise - together in the Temple. The newborn child had been brought to the Temple to fulfil the law's ritual requirements. At that moment the redemption of Israel was revealed to them.

Yet the glory of Israel was also to be a light to the Gentiles and the joy of a fulfilled promise came with the threat of an unacceptable compromise. This would be the true testing of the inner self of many, especially those who considered themselves religiously pure. Would their hearts be big enough for God's purpose? Or would tradition and sectarian hardness lead to the rejection of the very thing they longed for? Is it any different in our time, our culture and our church?

**PRAY**

Pray that we would joyfully accept the salvation God has provided. Pray that we would not impose our limits on God's salvation.

# Part 2
## MINISTERING IN GALILEE

Luke's story of Jesus' ministry begins with testimony. First, John identifies Jesus as the promised one. Then God himself, through the Spirit, names Jesus as his Son.

Jesus then returns to Galilee, in the North of Israel, to begin his public ministry. It is in Galilee that he declares to the people that in him God had fulfilled his promise. It is in Galilee that Jesus preaches, teaches and does miraculous acts.

Along the way he gathers the first of his new community - fishermen, tax-collectors, sinners, the poor, the despised and the ignored.

Luke makes clear that at the heart of Jesus' ministry is a declaration of authority - authority over sin, over illness and over the law. That declaration provokes two responses. His disciples, though slow and struggling at times, increasingly put their faith in him. His opponents - the leaders of the community - are increasingly hostile to him.

Conflict is growing; a clash is coming. As Jesus looks ahead to the final showdown in Jerusalem, the Father once more bears witness to the Son. The disciples are called to the self-sacrificing way of the cross. For those who would follow him to Jerusalem, there is no other option.

# 2  A PROMISE FULFILLED

## Faith in a vacuum?

*Luke 3:1-6, 19-20*

Another introduction, another list of unfamiliar names. Why? Simply because John's voice calling in the desert was not just an appeal to individual men and women to repent. It was a declaration that God was about to act to bring salvation to his world.

That declaration had implications for the local religious and political leaders, even for Caesar himself. They too were being addressed by the word of God. They too were being called to repent.

How did they react? They took God's prophet and threw him in prison. They represented order and stability. They represented power and authority. No preacher could be allowed to challenge that. But for Luke, Caesar was merely Caesar, God alone was Lord.

We are often tempted to live out our faith in a vacuum, isolated and safe from the world around us. God does not approve of faith in a vacuum. We are sent into the world to declare that he is Lord.

John could have stayed in the desert. John could have narrowed his focus. Instead he related the word to his world. It cost him his freedom and then his life.

## REFLECT

'Isolated and safe from the world around us.' Is this a description of your Christian faith?

(15)

**READING LUKE'S GOSPEL IN 50 DAYS**   *Luke 3:1-20*

## Good fruit or bad?

*Luke 3:7-14*

The crowds coming to John honoured Abraham as their father - they were the chosen people. Theirs was the covenant and the promise, the law and the prophets. God was their God. Now God had sent a prophet to proclaim the coming of his salvation.

Yet the message John brought was anything but comforting. John saw a people - his own people - who had received so much of God's grace. Yet instead of a humble spirit of praise he saw presumption, even pride. Instead of fruitful service he saw that the fruit was rotten on the tree.

John saw that these people - God's people - were as much in need of repentance as anyone else. Nor was repentance just a matter of saying the right words or being baptised. Repentance demanded change - a new lifestyle marked by service, honesty and integrity.

What would John say to Christians in Ireland? Have we ever been tempted to believe that we enjoy God's special favour? Would John expose our presumption? Would John point to our barrenness? Would he call us to repentance? And what would it mean for you and me to repent?

### REFLECT

Do Christians in this community have anything to repent of? Do you?

## What did you expect? *Luke 3:15-18*

John made an impact. He spoke with authority. He warned of judgement and called for repentance. People began to wonder. Could this be the deliverer promised by God?

During dark days in the past God had raised up leaders to deliver Israel - Moses, David, Elijah. Even better, God had promised another, greater, deliverer whose reign would never end. Dark days had come again when John the Baptist appeared. Could he be the one who would expel the Romans, put an end to corrupt religion and wickedness and restore Israel to glory?

They were wrong. John pointed them to another. Yet the tragedy was that when this other one came as John said he would, these people rejected him. Why? Because he did not fit their expectations. This was not how they believed God would act.

What are our expectations of how God should act? Often we seem quite sure of what God will do. Yet it is foolish to think that God will act only in the ways we expect. It is foolish to believe that God will fulfil his promises only in ways that we anticipate. How tragic it would be if our expectations of God were to blind us to God at work.

### PRAY

In your prayers today ask God for the vision to see what he is doing and the grace to accept it, even when it is not what you expect.

## Serve him only!

*Luke 4:1-13*

Jesus, anointed by the Spirit, was proclaimed the Son of God, the promised deliverer, the Messiah (3.21-22). Now the Spirit led him into the desert to be tested. What kind of Messiah would he be?

Providing for his own need, would he put himself before God? Would he seek to gain glory and power for himself in the world by compromising with the forces that control it? Would he test God's promise of protection?

If he had failed at any point his ministry was finished before it had started. However, Jesus rejected the way set before him in the desert, choosing instead the better way of absolute faithfulness to God.

He was tempted as we are, and we are tempted as he is. Temptations can be subtle - even reasonable. Sometimes they come with a word from the Bible. But the devil can take the truth of God and make it into a lie.

For Christians today the pursuit of power, whether in family, church or community presents a particularly dangerous temptation, even if we determine to use that power for good. But God wants our faithfulness and obedience. If we serve him he will provide the power we need.

**PRAY**

Pray today for those who have positions of power in our community. Pray that they would resist the temptation to use it wrongly.

**A PROMISE FULFILLED**

### Mercy moves on                              *Luke 4:16-30*

Isaiah looked forward to a great day (Isaiah 61.1-2). On that day God's deliverer would come. The needy, the outcasts and the oppressed would hear good news. The blind in eye and heart would see. Those captives of the evil one would be released. The year of the Lord's favour promised the cancellation of debts, promised forgiveness.

As Jesus spoke in the synagogue he revealed that he was that one, that the great day had come. What would they do? Accept him or reject him? They rejected him and rejected God's offer of salvation.

There were consequences. In earlier days the widows and lepers of Israel suffered because the people rejected God's prophets. Mercy moved on, crossing the political and ethnic borders, bringing salvation to the alien and the enemy.

Jesus' hearers got angry at this. Jesus was accusing them of rejecting God's anointed one. He was telling them that they were putting themselves outside the sphere of God's mercy and salvation.

The good news is still the same. God still works it out in ways we do not expect or understand. We can accept or reject what God is doing. But if we reject, mercy might move on.

**PRAY**

Give thanks to God for his mercy on our community. Ask that we and others would respond to his mercy before it is too late.

**READING LUKE'S GOSPEL IN 50 DAYS**    *Luke 4:31-44*

# ③ BREAKING BOUNDARIES

# day 1

## Follow me

*Luke 5:1-11, 27-32*

Could anyone be more compromised than a tax collector? Taking money from the people of God and handing it over to pagan Romans? As for fishermen, they were hardly an example of holy living. These people Jesus spoke with and ate with had crossed the boundary. They had compromised on purity, given up on faithfulness.

No wonder those who had remained faithful - the Pharisees - were offended. Worse still, Jesus wanted these sort of people to be his disciples. Had the man no standards?

Yes, Jesus had standards. It was just that the Pharisees did not understand them. Jesus' standard was the overflowing grace of God. Theirs was that grace too, but flowing within clearly bounded channels. For them, grace marked the boundary, keeping impurity and compromise out. For Jesus, grace marked the centre, out of which poured mercy great enough to smash through every border.

Christians, having experienced God's boundless grace, often give in to the temptation to draw new boundaries. Great time and effort goes into deciding who belongs and who does not.

Isn't it ironic that in our call to be disciples we identify with the sinners and tax collectors, while in our practice we so often behave like the Pharisees?

**REFLECT**

Think of some of the boundaries Christians in Ireland have put up. Would Jesus commend them or cross them?

# 3  BREAKING BOUNDARIES

## The company he keeps
*Luke 5:12-15; 7:36-50*

As if sinners and tax collectors weren't bad enough, Jesus also had time for lepers and prostitutes. Lepers did not mix in respectable company. They were out of sight and out of mind. As for prostitutes... But Jesus was willing to go to the very lowest rung of the social ladder and then step off.

Where others shunned the leper Jesus touched him. Was he corrupted or contaminated? No! His holiness drove out the leper's uncleanness (5.12-15).

And what of this woman? Intruding on the meal, she is an embarrassment. Her open display of love and gratitude is inappropriate. Moreover, if Jesus were a prophet he would know all about this woman and keep his distance (7.37-39).

Once more we see Jesus breaking down the boundaries that religious people had built in the name of God. The Pharisee with whom Jesus dined had, no doubt, done what he felt needed done, but much had been left undone. This women had gone far beyond what was needed. Great forgiveness provoked great love. Great love led to a wonderful extravagance.

Where would we modern day disciples have been? Hugging the leper or turning away? Weeping tears of gratitude at Jesus feet? Or muttering about the unseemliness and inappropriateness of it all?

**REFLECT**

Who is 'out of sight and out of mind' in your social circle? What could you do to welcome them in?

# BREAKING BOUNDARIES

## Love your enemies

*Luke 6:27-36*

Love your enemies, said Jesus. Everyone knew who he meant. The enemy was Rome - the politicians, soldiers and collaborators. The enemy was the other community - Samaritans mostly. The enemy was all around - political compromisers, religious unbelievers or wrong believers. Love them, Jesus said, even when they hate you. Love them, Jesus said, not just in what you say but in how you live. Words are not enough. Do good to them.

We prefer to love our own - those who are like us, those who belong, those who will love us back. So what, says Jesus. Loving your own is the human way, not God's. But loving God's way is a hard calling. Jesus' command to love our enemies might well mean being walked over, having our rights denied and our commitment abused. Yet why should we be surprised or shocked? Wasn't that the experience of Jesus himself?

Be merciful, Jesus says. Be merciful to British and Irish, to nationalist and unionist, to loyalist and republican, to resident and marcher, to the gracious and the bigoted. Be merciful, love your enemies, do good. This is the mark of true discipleship. God approves of this.

## REFLECT

Name your enemies.
Think of some ways
you could show
love to them.

## Security policy                                                      *Luke 6:43-49*

Goodness cannot be faked. We may fool our friends and neighbours. We may gain a reputation for godliness. We may call Jesus Lord, defend his cause, proclaim his word, but he sees through us. True goodness overflows from the heart. If the heart is not right, goodness is a sham. Jesus' call to love our enemies "exposes the hypocrisy, shallowness, and self-deceit of every externally paraded goodness." (John Nolland)

True goodness results from building on the right foundation - obedience to the words and commands of Jesus. Only then can we be sure that we will stand in the storm.

Many, perhaps most, of us know these words and commands. But many of us, having heard those words, are still building on the wrong foundations. The foundation might be career or family, it might be nation or community, it might be civil rights and freedoms. But when the storm comes we will not stand. And when everything is collapsing will we understand that we built on the wrong foundation?

In a community that talks at length of security, do we believe that true security is only to be found in obeying the words of Jesus?

### PRAY

Pray today that we would hear God's words in a new way and that we would build our lives on them.

## True to the faith

*Luke 7:1-10*

This centurion was a god-fearing man. Though not a convert to Judaism he respected the God of Israel. The locals appreciated him. They were willing to help him in a time of trouble.

This one is worthy, they said. They meant well, but gave themselves away. God may bless the Gentiles, they thought, but only those that are worthy.

Another delegation arrived. Hearing the centurion's message Jesus declared himself amazed, proclaiming the centurion a man of great faith. For this centurion saw the truth - Jesus had authority. As the centurion's words carried the authority of his superiors, so Jesus words carried the authority of God.

This Gentile, a seeker after the true God, understood Jesus better than the people of God. Theirs was the law and the covenant, they knew Jesus as teacher and healer, but ultimately they were blind to Jesus as the revealer of God and deaf to his word of command.

How often have we assumed that we alone are true to the faith, limiting the places were real faith may be found? How often has Jesus heard the stumbling pleas of men and women we pity and said "I have not found such great faith even among Christians in Ireland"?

## REFLECT

When we hear words of faith from unexpected sources are we suspicious or do we rejoice?

# WHO IS THIS JESUS?

## One of the family

*Luke 8:19-21*

We like to think of ourselves as rugged individualists, but we still need to belong. In Jesus' world belonging to family or community was more important still. Belonging provided security, a home, shared beliefs and values - family and community were sacred. Belonging provided a safe space in a threatening world. The greater the threat the more strongly people valued and defended the ties of family and community.

Yet there was a difficulty. Belonging required conforming. Those who belonged had to believe and say and do what was expected. They were not to let the side down. And, of course, belonging meant excluding others - especially those seen as a threat, an enemy not to be trusted.

However, Jesus did not conform. He did not deny or disown his family but he put those ties on another footing. His family included all who heard and obeyed his word. His family included the excluded, even the enemy.

Jesus will not allow us to give our highest allegiance to family and community. For the Christian, such loyalties are subordinated to the claims of the Kingdom of God. No longer 'them and us', in Jesus it is 'I and thou'. The dividing wall of hostility is broken down.

### PRAY

Pray today that God would give us strength to follow him even when it means upsetting those we care about.

**READING LUKE'S GOSPEL IN 50 DAYS**    *Luke 8:1-25*

## The threat of life

*Luke 8:26-39*

For years this man had been out of his mind, living naked in the city cemetery, so self-destructive he had to be chained and guarded. Now he was "sitting at the feet of Jesus, clothed and in his right mind" (35). The people should have been pleased. This man, once their neighbour, had been restored to health and restored to his community. Yet they were so afraid they asked Jesus to leave.

We can become accustomed to the presence of fear, violence and death. In a world of conflict we tend to reduce people to the categories of mad or sane, good or evil, them and us. This simplifies things, helping us know where we stand and what to think. We cope by excluding and expelling those we fear.

Yet when peace comes the methods of survival we have developed and grown comfortable and secure with become obsolete. A new future means change but change involves new relationships with people who were once 'mad' and 'chained'. Exclusion must become embrace. Rejection must become acceptance.

To us, like the people in this story, God's promise of new life, love and forgiveness can feel like a threat rather than a gift.

### REFLECT

As our society faces a time of change are you filled with hope or with fear?

## God is not bound

*Luke 9:28-36*

"Let us make three booths," said Peter, "not knowing what he said" (33). What was Peter trying to do? It seems that he was trying to fit this experience of Jesus into the understanding of God he already had.

Peter is not alone in this. We all are tempted to fit God into our expectations. We expect God to endorse our cause, sustain our view of the world and approve our cultural and political ambitions. We try to contain God within our institutions and traditions. In the end we create for ourselves a god who is neither living nor divine. This god is an idolatrous projection of our human fears. Yet we presume we are doing what God approves.

Peter's presumption was silenced by the voice of God. The frightened disciples were called to listen to Jesus as he made known the God who shattered their expectations (34-36).

The living, free, dynamic God whose glory is seen in the face of Jesus Christ will not be bound and gagged by us. Like Peter, we are instructed to be silent and to listen. God is his own interpreter. His living word will always shatter the personal and cultural restrictions we place on him.

### PRAY

Give praise to the 'living, free, dynamic God.' He will not be contained by us, but neither will he abandon us.

## The valley of despair

*Luke 9:37-10:5*

Peter would have preferred to stay on the mountain of revelation. But Jesus led the disciples down into the valley of despair where a child's body was seized and torn by the powers of death.

The disciples had yet to comprehend that true glory could only be displayed in surrender. Nor did they understand that the glory of the mountain could not be understood apart from the suffering of the valley and the way of the cross (44).

God did not bless the disciples with a display of his glory so that they could bask in it or hoard it for themselves. The biblical response to blessing is obedience, expressed in love for ourselves, our neighbours and even our enemies.

The broken body of this child can remind us of the sectarian convulsions of our society - in our worst moments possessed by sinister and destructive powers. Perhaps, like the disciples, we would rather experience the glory of the mountaintop than face this. Perhaps, like the disciples, in our encounter with evil we will discover our powerlessness (40). But perhaps that's where God wants us to start.

### PRAY

Pray that the glory of Jesus, the suffering servant, would be shown in your life today.

# 4   WHO IS THIS JESUS?

## What spirit you are of?

*Luke 9:51-56*

Even as Jesus journeyed to Jerusalem to give his life for the world, the ancient hostility between Jews and Samaritans flared up. The local residents of a Samaritan village would not receive Jesus. As a Jew on a pilgrimage to Jerusalem he was not welcome. Their animosity stirred up that of the disciples: "Lord do you want us to call fire from heaven and consume them?" (54)

Both groups exhibit stubborn and sectarian attitudes but Jesus' disciples display a self-righteous indignation willing to countenance the destruction of the enemy.

In the name of the highest good - rights, liberty, tradition, truth - we can justify the meanest attitudes and the deepest inhumanity. How easy it is to be blinded by our sense of moral superiority. How easy it is to become what we hate.

What is most disturbing about this story is the unquestioning assumption that heaven would provide the fire of judgement on these obstinate residents. Jesus' rebuke was unqualified: "You do not know what spirit you are of." (55)

Those words continue to reverberate through the hearts, homes and communities of Northern Ireland. We too need to decide what 'spirit' will control our lives.

## REFLECT

Why do we so often assume that other people deserve God's judgement, but not us?

# Part 3
## JOURNEYING TO JERUSALEM

"As the time approached, Jesus resolutely set out for Jerusalem." (9.51) In these chapters we travel with Jesus on a journey that will reach its climax on the cross. Along the way there are more miracles, more parables and more teaching.

Jesus is preparing his disciples for life in the new community that his death and resurrection will inaugurate. They are taught the demands and privileges of the disciple's life. They learn what it means to follow Jesus in mission. They are confronted with the cost of obedience to his words. They are instructed in the meaning of prayer, forgiveness and the Kingdom. They are warned of the dangers of wealth and possessions, of self-righteousness and complacency.

There are regular confrontations with the religious authorities. Jesus is unsparing in his criticisms. They are condemned for their blindness, their stubbornness, their hypocrisy, their refusal to accept those God has accepted. They are warned that the hour of decision has come, that they too will suffer the judgement of God.

As Jesus approaches Jerusalem conflict is growing and the outcome is inevitable. Repeatedly, he speaks of his approaching death. All who hear him must choose. Will they reject him or will they follow him?

## The expert's dilemma

*Luke 10:25-37*

The crunch question: How should we live in order to gain eternal life? Back came another question: What does the law say? He was an expert, he knew the answer - love God, love your neighbour. But it was not enough. "Who is my neighbour?" he asked. The expert wanted to talk about boundaries. Jesus told him a story that shattered them.

To this half-dead man, the guardians of Israel's religion should have been neighbours. They failed. Concerned to maintain their holiness, they passed by. Holiness had conquered mercy.

Then he began talking about a Samaritan! To us 'the Good Samaritan', to them the enemy. But the enemy became the neighbour and Jesus' audience was offended.

The expert asked, Who is my neighbour? Jesus told him to go and be a neighbour - not just to his own sort but to the one he knew as his enemy. Jesus told him to accept neighbourliness from those he rejected, those on the other side of the boundary.

There will always be boundaries. But we are fools to believe that God will honour them. There will always be them and us, but the one who is a neighbour to the enemy will inherit eternal life.

**REFLECT**

Consider the costly extravagance of the Samaritan's care. Do we love our neighbours with the same costly extravagance?

# 5  DISCERNING GOD AT WORK                    day 2

## One thing necessary                    *Luke 10:38-41*

The house must have been full. Not only Jesus, but the disciples, had arrived. Hospitality demanded that they be treated as honoured guests. No wonder Martha was in a state. Yet while Martha was driven to distraction with her preparations, Mary sat with Jesus listening. No wonder Martha was upset.

When Martha gave vent to her annoyance Jesus did not condemn her. Hospitality and service were good. Martha's desire was to honour the master. But she had become preoccupied, distracted. She had missed out on hearing Jesus and she was getting upset with her sister. Jesus gently suggested that what Martha needed was not her sister's help, but his words. Being taken up with Jesus is the one thing necessary.

We live in a world that values activity and achievement. Even our Christian traditions can put the emphasis on activity. Yet we too can become preoccupied. We too can end up critical of our brothers and sisters if they do not do things our way. We too can be left with no time to sit at the feet of Jesus and hear his word. And without that word, how can we be sure that in all our activity we are doing his will and glorifying him?

## REFLECT

In your fellowship and service how much time is spent doing and talking and how much time is spent listening to the words of Jesus?

## Hearts of darkness       *Luke 11:29-36*

Be careful what you take into your heart, says Jesus. If your heart is darkness, it will show. But if your heart is light, it will shine out to all.

In their continued resistance to Jesus and their constant demand for more signs, the crowd revealed the darkness of their hearts. Instead of accommodating the darkness they needed to let the light of Jesus shine in their hearts to chase the darkness out. Then the light would shine from them.

What lies within us? We encounter the darkness every day. We are surrounded by violence, greed, lust, anger, dishonesty, blasphemy, hate. We absorb it, and the darkness enters our hearts. In Northern Ireland we are surrounded by sectarian attitudes, religious prejudice, a culture of suspicion, an unforgiving spirit, spiritual pride. We absorb it, and the darkness enters our hearts.

And despite our good deeds and our fine words, our eyes do not shine with the light of Jesus. Do we think our neighbours don't see this? Christians in Northern Ireland need to resist the darkness and let the light of Jesus drive it from our hearts. Only then can we shine with the light of Jesus in our community.

**REFLECT**

To what extent are your attitudes shaped by the light of God's word and to what extent by the darkness of the world?

# ⑤ DISCERNING GOD AT WORK                    day 4

### Where is your treasure?                    *Luke 12:22-34*

Life is more than food and clothing. How true, we say,
with our full cupboards and wardrobes. But for Jesus'
disciples it was different. Life in Palestine was hard.
Poverty, disease and hunger were constant companions.

Yet we have our own worries - is my job secure, will
the mortgage rate go up, will my family hold together,
what will happen to our country and our community?
Worry damages our relationship with God for, like the
disciples, we can become people of little faith. Worry
also damages our relationships with others, for it brings
out the worst in us. We become suspicious and fearful of
others. We cling to what we have.

To us Jesus issues the same challenge: Where is your
treasure, where is your heart? Where do we find our
security, our identity and our hope? What really matters?
Is it our family, our career, our denomination, our political
allegiance?

Jesus says, find your security in God, trust in him,
do not worry. More than this, he says, let your trust
in God produce generosity and graciousness to those
around you. Trust in God frees us to treasure the
relationships that are at the centre of life: relationships
with God, with our neighbour - and with our enemy.

**PRAY**
Pray that we would
be people whose
security and
confidence
is in God.
Pray too that he
would make us
generous people
with our neighbours.

### Signs of the times

*Luke 12:49-59*

Life depended on the harvest. The harvest depended on the weather. Little wonder these people took time to read the signs in the sky. Sometimes the signs were hopeful; at other times, ominous.

There were other signs too - signs of the times. Jesus' words and deeds were signs of the Kingdom. For some they brought hope, freedom, salvation. For others they were ominous, dark and threatening. Still others were blind, blissfully unaware of God at work in their midst.

Jesus' words challenged their complacency. The Prince of Peace was also the judge of all. His call forced men and women to decide - for the Kingdom or against the Kingdom. There was no third way. The cost might be division and conflict. But there was no escaping the decision.

What's more, time was running out. They were like people on their way to court. If they wanted to escape the fire of judgement there was not a moment to waste.

We believe God is judge, but usually we believe that judgement will fall on others. Could it be that we too have misread the signs of the times? Are we the ones being dragged off to the judge?

### REFLECT

Is time running out for the church in this land? Or might it already be too late?

### Sort yourself out!                                    *Luke 13:1-8*

What was going on when Pilate and his forces of occupation butchered the Galileans? What about those who shot, maimed and killed people in thirty years of terrorism? Are they to become Christians and be forgiven, while their victims go to hell? The difficult questions need to be asked. The problem is that while we indulge ourselves in struggling with the difficult questions, we avoid dealing with the obvious ones.

There is no rebuke from Jesus for asking difficult questions, nor is there any attempt to exonerate God from moral culpability. Quite the reverse. What about the Siloam eighteen? asks Jesus. Were they any worse than anyone else? Jesus doesn't try and map out the workings of providence. Instead, he forces his questioners to face the challenge of the values of the Kingdom for themselves. Stop trying to sort out the wrongs of others and deal with your own, he tells them.

In Jerusalem, Jesus says, he sees little spiritual or moral improvement. God would be quite entitled to pull the whole place down. The wonder of God's mercy is that he's prepared to dig around and fertilise the fruitless fig-tree so that it might yet produce the fruit of repentance. How long must he dig around us?

**PRAY**

Pray today for the wisdom to ask the right questions, the openness to hear God's response and the grace to change.

## Unclean and unshaven        *Luke 13:18-19*

The significance of the parable of the mustard seed lies in the fact that the birds of the air are welcome. It's true that there are other important lessons to be drawn from the parable, but let's make sure we don't miss this one.

The Old Testament tells us that the eagle, the vulture, the raven, the gull and a host of other birds are to be considered unclean by the Israelites. Even to touch the carcass of one of these birds, never mind to eat one, is to make oneself unclean. For the sake of purity the distinctions of kind must be observed.

Speaking to an audience who observed these rules, Jesus teaches them that as far as this mustard tree - the Kingdom of God - is concerned, these distinctions no longer count. The Kingdom of God is for everyone.

There is no longer any distinction between the clean and the unclean. The wild is as welcome as the domesticated. The predator is as welcome as the victim. The vulture and the sparrow roost together in the Kingdom. 'Aramis man' and the unshaven are both welcome in God's Kingdom. But, are both welcome in our churches?

**REFLECT**

Put yourself in the shoes of someone who does not 'fit' in your church. How can your church become a place where that person can feel welcome?

## A little goes a long way

*Luke 13:20-21*

You buy it in little sachets and mix it in with the flour. Make up a one and a half pound batch of flour and then add one sachet of yeast. It only weighs about a quarter of an ounce. That represents around one per cent of the whole mixture. But that's enough to transform a sticky mess of dough into a delicious plain loaf.

It's not the quantity of the yeast that matters. What matters is that the yeast is a different kind of substance. So too is the Kingdom of God. The Kingdom of God permeates and transforms humanity. But its effectiveness is not dependent on power and influence. Its strength is not in force of numbers, military might or semtex. The Kingdom of God transforms through righteousness and godliness.

Yeast is known as a raising agent. The church should be a raising agent, permeating every part of the community without distinction and without exception. Yeast in the dough knows no borders or boundaries. Neither should the raising agent of the Kingdom.

### PRAY

Pray that God would make his church effective in permeating our community with the values of his Kingdom.

## Good living for a living      *Luke 14: 15-24*

It had been a difficult meal. Respectable people were present, formalities were being observed. Jesus had healed an unclean man. Embarrassing enough in itself, but it was Sabbath and healing was work. Then Jesus, the guest, began to lecture the host, a prominent Pharisee.

Someone had to change the subject and someone did. It was one of those nauseating pious comments, What really counts is being at the banquet in heaven, Amen! Wouldn't you agree Jesus?

Jesus' response was devastating. If you want to keep the Sabbath and demonstrate your holiness, he said, then go and break a few of your own self imposed rules. Break down the barriers, cross the social boundaries. Stop seeing the outsider, the outcast, the other side as irredeemable and unworthy. Get them round your dinner table, get rid of these pious cronies. Your pious friends, said Jesus, are more interested in their land, their money and their sex lives than the Kingdom of God - good living for a living.

The pious selfish ones at the centre of the action and at the top of the table might just find there is no invitation to the party in heaven. Isn't that right Mr. Pharisee?

**REFLECT**

If you were drawing up a guest list for a dinner party who would you invite? And what would Jesus make of your choice?

## Noses out of joint                        *Luke 15:11-32*

"This man welcomes sinners and eats with them"(2). You can hear the disgust, the superiority, the 'shock horror' in their voices. That's the context for this story of the father with the big soft heart.

This shameless and vulgar boy had brought shame on his family and community. You have to draw the line somewhere, they would have said. Some behaviour is intolerable. This lad has gone too far.

Wild living, squandering the land and working with pigs put him beyond the bounds of forgiveness. Being a Lundy, fraternising with the enemy or doing time means you've fallen on the wrong side of the bounds of acceptability.

The Father of the Kingdom works differently. Having set the bounds of holiness and acceptable behaviour, he goes to the boundary to wait - not for judgement - but for signs of repentance. His joy is found, not in the punishment of the disrespectful, but in the return of the prodigal.

Do we sit on the boundary to watch the judgement fall, or do we prepare the celebration for the returning prodigal? Are our noses out of joint when the Father forgives? If they are we are no better children of the Father than the profligate prodigal.

**REFLECT**

We have all come to the Father as prodigals, but have we become like the Father or the elder brother?

## That's not fair!

*Luke 17:1-10*

Begging forgiveness seven times in the one day. How could this be sincere? But Jesus says forgive.

Traditionally the burden was on the guilty to prove their sincerity. Our tradition is much the same. In our community both forgiveness and repentance have been thin on the ground. I will forgive when they repent, we say. But Jesus says forgive.

Forgiveness is not a matter of calculation, not a matter of procedure. What Jesus requires of us is "a capacity to forgive that knows no limits and gives all the benefit of the doubt to the sinner." (John Nolland)

If we are unable to forgive perhaps we have yet to grasp the full significance of Jesus' words. Or perhaps our theological objections hide the unforgiving spirit within. And if we claim that we cannot forgive because we see no true repentance, does it pain us? Is it our deepest desire to be able to forgive?

No wonder the disciples called for a greater faith. Yet the faith they had was sufficient, for it tapped into the power of the Kingdom. Besides, said Jesus, a forgiving spirit is not a sign of great spirituality or piety. It is a basic part of our duty towards God as we serve him.

### PRAY

Ask God today to make us people who long to forgive and who rejoice in forgiving.

### Don't walk away

*Luke 17:11-19*

Lepers were rejected by their families and feared by their communities. With Jesus these ten found hope, one who would not walk away or reject them. Yet it was only as they obeyed his command and walked away that they were healed. On the way to see the priest, life changed for all of them.

But only one, a Samaritan, returned to give glory to God and thanks to Jesus. All ten were freed from leprosy but only the Samaritan found salvation because of his faith in Jesus.

The power of the Kingdom of God had been at work in all of them, but only one made the right response of faith and gratitude.

How would we have responded to these social, political and ethnic rejects? When they called out, Jesus heard them. When they approached, Jesus met with them. When they asked for help, Jesus served them. When the one showed his faith, Jesus accepted and affirmed him.

How do we respond to the outsiders in our community? Do we hear them when they call out? Are we willing to serve them? And where we see faith in the Son of God do we affirm it and rejoice?

**PRAY**

Praise God that he hears us when we cry out to him. Pray that we would be people who hear the cries of the outsiders.

## Piety or penitence?

*Luke 18:9-14*

To us, Pharisees are models of self-righteousness and hypocrisy. To Jesus' hearers they were models of piety and 'good living'. Tax-collectors, on the other hand, were scum. Unless we see this we miss the point.

The Pharisee starts well: "God, I thank you" (11). This man was not unaware that only God's grace made him different from the tax-collector. But his pursuit of righteousness had become the basis for judging and excluding those who did not measure up. This Pharisee had built barriers between himself and others on the basis of his righteousness and their lack of it.

The tax-collector had nothing to offer God but his unworthiness and sin. His penitence might impress us, but, like the Pharisee, we would probably have suspected that he had much to be penitent for.

However, Jesus' words turned their world inside out. The loathsome tax collector was accepted by God. The pious Pharisee was not.

How do we see ourselves in this story? As the humble penitent, throwing ourselves on God's mercy? How do others in our community see us Christians? Good living, upright people whose righteousness is a barrier that judges and excludes them? How does God see us? When he speaks his word of judgement will we be exalted or will we be humbled?

**REFLECT**

Have Christians turned grace – God's gift of inclusion – into a barrier of exclusion?

## Do you not understand                    *Luke 18:31-34*

Jesus was heading for disaster. He was on a collision course with the leaders of the Jewish people. At every turn his words and actions had challenged and rebuked them. Their vision was one of exclusiveness, of a community shaped and defined by boundaries.

Jesus shattered their boundaries, crossed their borders and reached out to those excluded and suspected. He offered repentance and forgiveness where they offered only judgement and rebuke.

Jesus' challenge to the religious status quo had political consequences too. His message threatened the established order. Something had to be done.

Yet the disciples still did not understand the implications of Jesus' ministry. Was it because they had failed to understand fully the implications of what Jesus was doing? Were they still trying too hard to make Jesus fit into something they knew and understood? Were they looking to domesticate this message and make it more comfortable, more realistic?

Christians in Northern Ireland are 'boundary' people. We draw, or let others draw, boundaries that separate us from each other, our community from the other community. Jesus crosses boundaries now as surely as he did then. And like the disciples we don't fully understand the message, and we don't fully understand the implications of the message. And if we did what would it mean for this community?

**PRAY**

Give thanks to God for the insight we have into the implications of the gospel. Pray that we will continue to grow in our understanding of its implications.

## Dirty beggars!                                    *Luke 18:35-43*

Even a blind beggar knew there was something going on. Jesus of Nazareth was passing by with the crowd in tow. "Mercy," was his cry. "Shut up," was their response. Something big was happening. This was no time to bother Jesus with small concerns, let alone with the small concerns of a beggar.

But Jesus had time for the beggar. The one excluded by the crowd was called into Jesus' presence. The one who had been told to shut up by the crowd talked with Jesus.

He wanted to see and his persistent, determined faith brought him to the one who could make him well. Jesus spoke and it was done. No longer blind, no longer an outsider, the beggar took his place as a follower of Jesus, praising God.

Who are the beggars in our community? Who gets pushed to the margins, whose voice goes unheard, even when they cry out to Jesus? Is it those with whom we differ politically or doctrinally? Or is it those whose morals we dislike - the divorced, single parents, homosexuals, beggars, drunkards, criminals, terrorists?

Jesus hears the cry for mercy of all those to whom we are deaf and indifferent or even hostile. But do they find mercy through us or despite us?

**REFLECT**

Do people find Jesus despite us or because of us?

# Part 4
## AS ONE WHO SERVES

As Jesus enters Jerusalem there are mixed emotions. The crowds are cheering and praising God. The religious authorities are angered at this unseemly behaviour. Jesus himself is weeping for the city that, despite the cheers, has rejected him and in rejecting him has rejected the hope of peace. For them, the future holds only destruction and chaos.

At the Temple Jesus issues his most direct challenge yet to the authorities. Their response is to try and trap him in debate. But, unable to win the argument, they resort to other means. As Jesus and his followers meet for Passover, Judas goes about his business of betrayal.

After the arrest Pilate, Herod and the religious establishment join forces to get rid of this troublemaker. A crowd cheered his arrival, now a crowd demands his execution. Yet even in death Jesus offers the hope of forgiveness to the dying thief.

The rulers go home satisfied. But this is not the end. Something has happened. The tomb is empty. Jesus is meeting with his followers. And as he is taken up into heaven, they wait on God to fulfil another promise - the promise of the Spirit. In his power they will continue the mission of Jesus, proclaiming repentance and forgiveness of sins to all nations.

# TRUE ALLEGIANCE

## Actions speak louder than words

*Luke 19:1-10*

Jericho was a bustling commercial centre in Jesus' day. As an unscrupulous tax collector, Zacchaeus would have been well off. Despite his wealth, though, he was despised by his community.

When Jesus came visiting the crowds flocked to him. Zacchaeus, too, was curious. Unable to see, he chose an unusual vantage point. The encounter that followed resulted in a conversation that caused a scandal.

Jesus refused to see Zacchaeus as a criminal or an outcast. He saw instead a person to be known and enjoyed. This attitude did not go down well. Nor was it only the religious types who muttered about Jesus' shocking behaviour (7).

Zacchaeus' response was astonishing. Half his wealth went to the poor. The rest went to provide restitution - far beyond the requirements of the Law - to those he had wronged. Jesus, in turn, recognised that his actions revealed his heart. Here, truly, was a son of Abraham.

Zacchaeus did not belong and was not wanted by his community, but he mattered to Jesus. There are many in our community too who are unwanted and rejected - paramilitaries, republicans, loyalists, prisoners, murderers. But they matter to Jesus.

**PRAY**

Think of the people who do not belong in your circle. Now think of them as people who matter to Jesus. Pray for them as you pray for yourself today.

# 8  TRUE ALLEGIANCE

### Cheers and complaints

*Luke 19:28-40*

To say that Jesus was not political is to say that Jesus was not human. Born and raised in a culture of oppression, his people knew the reality of persecution. Jesus, too, would have felt the searing indignation of Israel at the injustice of their plight.

Now, approaching Jerusalem, Jesus revealed himself as Israel's true and only king. Zechariah prophesied that Israel's king would come riding on a colt (Zechariah 9.9). Now he had come. The crowds rejoiced, spreading their cloaks before him, a 'red carpet' for their king.

But not all rejoiced. The blindness of the Pharisees was even greater than that of the stones of the fields. Once again they had shown their inability to see the signs of the times.

Yet the cheers of many soon turned to hostility. A king he was, but not the sort they wanted. He came in peace on a donkey, not as a military conqueror. His was the way of sacrifice. His was the way of peace. This was not what they wanted from their king.

If Jesus were displaying his identity in Belfast today, would we be irritated or would we cheer? And if his way of sacrifice and of peace began to unsettle us, would we still be cheering?

### PRAY

Pray that we would be true followers and obedient subjects of the king of peace.

# 8  TRUE ALLEGIANCE                              day 3

### It all ends in tears                          *Luke 19:41-44*

Jesus wept tears of regret and pity as he looked out over the city of Jerusalem. As the King, coming in peace and motivated by love, he could have saved this people and their city. Instead, he foresaw the tragedy to come when Jerusalem would be utterly destroyed. On that day the city would lie like a ploughed field. Not three but thousands of crosses would stand outside the ruined walls as the Romans took revenge for Jewish rebellion.

Why did it happen? "Because you did not recognise the time of God's coming to you" (44). The judgement of God is a terrifying thing - not so much because of its mechanics as because of its finality.

In Ireland Christ has come to us through centuries of teaching and tradition. There have been startling examples of some who have selflessly followed the master's lead. But others have taken for themselves a position not rightfully theirs.

Assuming God was on their side, imagining his will accorded with theirs, they considered others beyond the pale, treating them as second class and spiritually inferior. This was the path travelled by the Jewish people in New Testament times and the judgement of God fell upon them.

**REFLECT**

When Jesus looks upon Belfast does he smile with pleasure at the obedience of a faithful people or does he weep tears of regret at what might have been?

## Woe to the vessel!

*Luke 20:9-19*

It seemed clear enough. The tenants had rejected the owner's servants and murdered his son. Israel had rejected God's prophets and were conspiring to murder God's son. Yet the people could not imagine such a thing. May this never be!

But the scriptures were clear. What Israel rejected, God had honoured. Jesus was the capstone - the key to the whole. More than this he was the stone on which they would perish. "If a vessel falls upon a stone woe to the vessel. If a stone falls upon the vessel woe to the vessel." So said Israel's rabbis. Here Jesus made the same point. When one comes up against the other the vessel is destroyed.

The son's death might have seemed like the tenants' victory, but it sealed their fate. Ultimately, their evil ways would be dealt with. God takes the long view. Woe to the vessel.

Every time someone is killed, every time a bomb explodes, every time a grieving widow is comforted, every time our conflict is branded a religious war we may be inclined to think that evil is having its way unrestrained.

But, ultimately, the vessel will come against the stone. And on that day woe to the vessel.

### PRAY

While praying today, affirm your faith in a God who knows what he is doing and who takes the long view.

## 8  TRUE ALLEGIANCE

### Giving Caesar his due

*Luke 20:20-26*

The poll tax symbolised Rome's authority over Israel. Faithful Jews proclaimed that God alone was Israel's king. What were they to do when the Roman Emperor made the rules?

In the hands of Jesus' enemies this concern became the basis of a trick question. Where did his loyalties lie? Jesus responded that having accepted Caesar's currency, they were bound to accept Caesar's right to impose taxes.

However, having acknowledged Caesar's authority, Jesus placed it under the authority of God. There was a point at which Caesar's authority stopped. But God's authority was absolute.

What does this mean for Christian citizens? Should we seek to transform the world, seeing it as the property of Christ? Or should we divorce ourselves from it, seeing it as a wreck from which people must be plucked? Jesus suggests that involvement is not only necessary but appropriate, for God had not given up his authority over the state to Caesar.

Christian citizens should act prophetically before those who legislate on our behalf, bringing to bear upon them the full force of the values of God's Kingdom revealed in his word. As William Barclay put it, "The Christian is at once the servant and the conscience of the state."

**REFLECT**

Are you a citizen of this country who happens to be a Christian, or are you a Christian citizen?

**READING LUKE'S GOSPEL IN 50 DAYS**    *Luke 20:27-47*

## When God moves

*Luke 21:1-6*

The Temple, wrote Josephus - a Jewish historian of the first century - stood above Jerusalem like a "snow clad mountain." It was big and it was beautiful - even the Romans were impressed. It spoke of security, stability, permanence. More than that, it spoke of the greatness of Israel's God and Israel's status as his people. No wonder the disciples were impressed.

Jesus' response turned their world upside down. They saw security and permanence. Jesus foresaw chaos and destruction. No longer a snow clad mountain, the site of the Temple would become a wasteland. The beautiful stones they admired would be thrown down.

God was moving on. The Temple had fulfilled its purpose. Now, God was present in the one who stood by their side speaking with them. Yet for all the time they had spent with him they were still attached to what was familiar.

Do we have the insight to see that sometimes God moves on? Or are we tempted to cling to the formulas, places and practices of the past? Once, perhaps, God was present in and worked through these things. But just because God was there once does not mean he is there now. Are we willing to leave behind familiar comfortable ways when God does something new?

**PRAY**

Pray today for the wisdom to know when God is moving on and the grace to follow him.

# 9 FATEFUL DECISIONS

day 2

## Tradition betrayed

*Luke 22:1-6*

Passover was coming. Jews from around the world were gathering in Jerusalem to celebrate God's deliverance of their ancestors from slavery in Egypt.

The leaders of the people were preoccupied - but not with celebration. Passover was a time of tension. After all, it was a celebration of liberation and freedom. It was an ideal opportunity to stir up people against the Romans. And now there was this man Jesus, hugely popular with the people.

The religious leaders needed to find a way to get rid of him. There was too much at stake to leave this loose cannon roaming the city freely. Then Judas came with his offer of betrayal. Now they celebrated.

Who would have believed it? Jesus was the fulfilment of all the exodus deliverance represented. Jesus was God's new deliverer. Yet even as they remembered God's grace in the past they were blind to the presence of God's grace among them.

Like them we know our history. Like them we remember the times of God's deliverance and mercy. But like them history and memory have blinded us. Our adherence to our tradition has triumphed over a living faith that recognises God at work.

**PRAY**

Pray that God would give us eyes to see our history and traditions in a way that enlightens us. Pray that we would not be blinded by them.

### Authority to serve
*Luke 22:24-30*

How many of us looking through the window of a restaurant aspire to be a waiter rather than a diner? Doubtless we would prefer to sit back and enjoy the meal. But Jesus reminds his disciples that he is the one doing the waiting. So it is with the Kingdom of God.

Greatness, as the disciples understood it, was about power, position and authority. Greatness, as Jesus understood it, was about humility, service and self-giving.

All of us seek power in some way. But for those in positions of authority the challenge is particularly difficult. In business, in politics, even in the church, an attitude of humility and service does not come easily. Yet this is what Jesus demanded and this is where true greatness will be found.

To live this way might make us look foolish and weak. It might leave us vulnerable to accusations of surrender. It might annoy those whose constant demand is for the satisfaction of their rights.

Nonetheless, it is only to those who follow the example of Christ in humble service that the promise of a seat at the table in the Kingdom of God is given. Humble service now will be rewarded with great honour and great authority then.

### PRAY
Pray for those who hold positions of power. Pray that they would exercise power with humility and service.

## 9  FATEFUL DECISIONS

### Your will be done

*Luke 22:39-46*

Jesus had made this journey many times and with the same purpose, to spend time with his Father. However this was a night like no other, the future of humanity was at stake.

The honesty of his prayer is striking. If at all possible he would rather not face the horrors that lay ahead. Even angelic strengthening did not diminish his anguish. Yet he committed himself to take from his Father's hand the cup that would cost him everything and bring us deliverance.

The sorrow of suffering drove Jesus to prayer. But the reaction of the disciples lies in startling contrast. They had heard Jesus' instruction to pray so that they would not fall into temptation. But sorrow immobilised them and they were overcome by sleep.

How often have the sorrows of our community overwhelmed us? How often, when they should have driven us to prayer, have they left us paralysed? How often have we given in to the temptation to give up, to run away, to avoid the suffering?

Could it be that Jesus is shaking us awake? Perhaps he wants us to turn our suffering and sorrow into intense and deep engagement with our Father in prayer.

**REFLECT**

Do we pray for our community in its suffering with the same intensity and passion as Jesus? Or have we given up?

## I will never deny you! *Luke 22:31-34, 54-62*

Jesus' warning to Peter must have seemed incomprehensible. Here was a man ready to die for Jesus. However, a few hours later he is weeping bitter tears. The dawn is breaking but it is Peter's darkest hour.

What had happened to him? Perhaps the arrest of Jesus, his refusal to hit back, had left Peter dazed and confused. Now what? Still he followed, but at a distance. But there could be no following at a distance. "You also are one of them," someone said. It was Yes or No. Peter said No.

Jesus' look brought bitter sorrow, but it also put him back on the road to recovery. Though Peter had failed Jesus, God used that failure to strengthen Peter.

There are many ways to deny Jesus. Indeed, our lips can confess him even while our lives deny him. In Northern Ireland many have confessed with their lips. But have the lives of some of us been a denial?

But Jesus has prayed for us, that our faith will survive even though we stumble. And as the piercing look of Jesus drives us to tears, that look gives the grace of renewal. Reflecting on our denial we are strengthened in our faith and we strengthen one another.

### REFLECT

Think of some of the ways in which Christians in Ireland have denied Jesus. Ask God for the grace of renewal.

# 10 REJECTION & AFFIRMATION                    day 1

## The unholy alliance                          *Luke 23:1-12*

Jesus' vision was of a kingdom greater than any nation. No passport was needed, no badge of language or religion or culture, just a willing acceptance of his rule.

It was too much. "We have found this man subverting our nation," they cried (2). Even 2,000 years ago there were those who valued the nation more than the Kingdom. So Jesus, whose radical challenge to their loyalties was so disturbing, had to pay a price.

The crowd that once cheered now demonstrated their love for their nation by denouncing their king to their enemy. And those whose authority was based on power and might formed an unlikely and unhealthy alliance to destroy Jesus.

As Dorothy Sayers put it, "The people who hanged Christ never accused Him of being a bore; on the contrary they thought Him too dynamic to be safe. Officialdom felt the established order of things would be more secure without Him. So they did away with God in the name of peace and quietness."

How many unhealthy - unholy - alliances have been formed in our land in pursuit of our own interests? And have we subverted Christ's Kingdom because we love our nation to much?

## REFLECT

Would an outsider, looking at Christians in Ireland, conclude that the Kingdom is more valuable to us than the nation?

### Time to choose

*Luke 23:13-25*

The people had a choice. They could choose Jesus and his kingdom of peace, justice and reconciliation. Or they could choose Barrabas, the nationalist fighter, and his kingdom of conflict, violence and exclusion. The people had a choice. They chose Barabbas. There was no justice in what happened. If Jesus really was innocent, he should have been acquitted and released.

People still have a choice. We can choose Christ and his Kingdom. Or we can choose the way of Barrabas. Not that we would want to support conflict or violence or exclusion - any more than the good people of Jerusalem did. But still we have to choose.

Jesus or my community? Jesus or my tradition? Jesus or my denomination? Community, tradition and denomination demand our allegiance. So does Jesus. And this is our choice - will we accommodate Jesus to our tradition or will we surrender all to Jesus and his Kingdom?

And what irony in the end! Nobody really wants Barrabas. After all, what would the decent people of Jerusalem want with a terrorist? In the same way the decent people of Belfast would never want to justify murder in the name of God!

**REFLECT**

Pray today that God's will would inform all our decisions. Pray that we would be enabled to choose the way of Jesus whatever the cost.

## It's scandalous!

*Luke 23:39-48*

Rulers sneered, soldiers mocked. One criminal abused him, the other cried out to him. The crowd that had once cheered his arrival and then demanded his death, now drifted away in despair and anguish. His followers stood at a distance, while a lone Roman soldier spoke the truth. In his death as much as in his life Jesus was a stumbling block.

From the Greek word for stumbling block we get our word 'scandal'. The gospel of Jesus was - and is - a scandal. His gospel tripped up the pious, shaking them out of their self-assurance. His gospel offended the guardians of righteousness, for he proclaimed it to the unrighteous and the despised.

The gospel of Jesus is still a scandal, for it refuses to be bound by our prejudices and judgements. It offers forgiveness where forgiveness seems so unfair. It pours out grace on those we consider insufficiently penitent.

Too often, we are as scandalised by the gospel as anyone else. But Jesus wants his followers to be stumbling blocks, tripping up the complacent and self-righteous in our own community. True disciples are accomplices in the scandal.

**REFLECT**

Churches are often accomplices in the status quo. Might God consider this to be a scandalous state of affairs?

REJECTION & AFFIRMATION        day 4

## I don't believe you!

*Luke 24:1-12*

These were brave woman. This was, after all, the tomb of an executed criminal they were visiting. The other disciples, whether from fear or despair, were nowhere to be seen.

However, nothing could have prepared them for the shock of discovery. The tomb was empty, heaven's messenger announced Jesus' resurrection. These first witnesses of Jesus' resurrection then witnessed to the other disciples.

And so the scandal continued. In Palestinian society a woman's testimony was not credible, but it was to these women that the messenger of God announced the good news of the resurrection. Sadly, the disciples did not think their testimony credible, dismissing it as nonsense.

We know that Jesus included the sinners and the tax-collectors, but sometimes we forget that he included other marginalised people - not least women and children.

Have Christians in Northern Ireland failed to hear the voices of those in our community whom God might be using to testify to us? Have we dismissed as 'nonsense' the words of women, of the children, of the poor? And in closing our minds and ears to them, have we closed our minds and ears to the voice of God?

**REFLECT**

Who is marginalised in our community or in your church? Do you believe they might have something to say you need to hear?

## He is risen!                                    *Luke 24:13-35*

These disciples had put their hope in Jesus, but Jesus had failed to do what they expected. And so their hope gave way to sorrow and despair.

Despair could have given way to the cynicism that expects only the worst and that takes pleasure in being proved right. Or they might have concluded that God needed a helping hand. Worse still, they might have put their hope in their own strength, fighting, even killing, for God.

But Jesus changed them. As they broke bread together the risen Jesus made himself known to them. They were transformed. Hope blazed anew. No longer tired, they rushed back to Jerusalem to spread the good news. Jesus is risen!

Where is your hope? Is it in your religion, your theology or your denomination? Is it in your family, your business or your money? Is it in your history, your culture or your community? Or has hope disappeared? As you look around you do you feel sorrow, despair, cynicism, anger, even hatred?

For many in our community hope is in short supply. Yet the church at this time must embody the hope of a new future, a new community in which we learn to recognise the risen, living Jesus when he speaks to us on the road of new beginnings.

**PRAY**

Pray today for those who have lost hope. Pray that God would make you a beacon of hope for them.

# Prayer

## Day 1

## Making Peace

God, as a people set apart for you,
we confess that we have neglected
to follow Jesus in the path of peace.
That our words and acts have at times
perpetuated fear and suspicion
and fuelled our sectarian conflict.
Help us to be peacemakers in our divided community.
To guard our words when we speak.
To overcome hostility with openness and love.
To cultivate skills to resolve conflict
And to value the gift of peace when we find it in others.
God let the peace of your son rule in our hearts.

Amen

# Prayer

## Day 2

### Bringing Healing

God, as a people set apart,
you have called us to be witnesses
to the good news of your
reconciling love in Jesus Christ.
A love that is both for the healing of our hearts
And the healing of the nations.
Help us to build relationships of love and
trust in our community.
And to overcome fear and hostility
with forgiveness and compassion.

Amen.

# Prayer

### Day 3

### Doing Justice

God, you have set us apart
as citizens of your kingdom
in which righteousness and justice reign.
Yet we confess that at times we only see
the injustices against ourselves
and are solely concerned with our rights.
But you require of us the courage
to embrace the hurt and loss of others
and the grace to listen to their story.
Help us to create a space for them,
to act justly and to love mercy,
and to walk humbly with you.

Amen

# Prayer

## Day 4

## Creating Hope

God, you have called us to be a sign of hope
in the face of apathy and despair.
We thank you that you have not abandoned our world
to the chaos and violence of human greed.
But your Holy Spirit continues to brood
over your good creation,
calling us out of darkness
and promising us new life and hope in Jesus Christ.
Help us to discern the small and vital signs
of your persistent presence transforming our broken
world.
God our hope is in you
and you have promised that we will not be disappointed.

Amen

# Prayer
## Day 5

## Witness in a Divided Community

Lord God,
As part of the body of Christ in this land
you have called us out of the world as a holy people
that we might be sent into the world as salt and light.
Forgive us that our witness has often lacked credibility
as we have failed to match our words with our attitudes
and actions.
We pray that your Spirit will renew your Church
in its witness to the reconciling love of Christ in this divided
community.
Help us:
To make peace, as we walk in the footsteps of the Prince
of Peace,
To bring healing, as we share the saving power of the
Healer of Nations,
To do justice, as we live under the authority of the Judge of
the Earth,
And to create hope, as we bear witness to the Christ in us
who is greater than he who is in the world.

Amen

# Luke's World

## Politics , Religion, Society

Though Palestine was part of the Roman Empire, for the most part it was ruled by local leaders who were loyal to Rome. Only in Judea and Samaria did the Romans rule directly. The two most important rulers mentioned in the gospel are Herod and Pontius Pilate.

*Herod*: Luke mentions two rulers called Herod. The first (1.5) died shortly after Jesus' birth and his kingdom was divided among four sons. One of these, also called Herod by Luke, ruled in Galilee throughout the period of Jesus' ministry.

*Pontius Pilate*: Another of the four sons was made ruler of Judea and Samaria but was later deposed by the Romans. They replaced him with a Roman governor. At the time of Jesus' ministry the governor was Pontius Pilate.

*The Council*: Luke also refers to 'the council of the elders' (22.66). This group had wide ranging powers in Judea, especially in legal matters. Members were drawn from priestly families, the local aristocracy and legal experts. It was chaired by the high-priest who was the most important religious and political figure in Jewish society.

*Temple and Synagogue*: The Temple was at the heart of Israel's life. It was a place of sacrifice, worship, teaching and pilgrimage. Local communities were centred on the synagogue. It was a place of teaching, prayer and education.

*Pharisees*: Pharisees believed that Israel needed to be transformed by living more fully according to the law. Those who did not seek to live by the law were condemned as sinners. Jesus' willingness to challenge their boundaries and meet with sinners provoked repeated disputes.

*Samaritans*: Samaritans were rejected by Jews because they were compromised religiously and ethnically. They had intermarried with non-Jews and they had a different understanding of the Jewish Scriptures.

*Sinners and Tax-collectors*: For Jesus' opponents sinners meant those who did not keep the law. In particular, it meant those who did not keep the law as his opponents understood it. Sinners defined those who were considered outside the bounds of acceptable religious belief and practice. Tax-collectors were particularly despised because they did Rome's dirty work. More than this, they often took an extra share for themselves.

# Contributors

All contributors are members of ECONI's Steering Group

**David Bruce**
General Secretary of Scripture Union

**David McMillan**
Pastor, Windsor Baptist Church, Belfast

**Gary Mason**
Minister, Sandy Row & Springfield Road Methodist, Belfast

**Heather Morris**
Minister, Dundonald Methodist

**Derek Poole**
ECONI Development Officer

**David Porter**
ECONI Director

**Steve Stockman**
Dean of Residence, Presbyterian Chaplaincy QUB

**Priscilla Reid**
Christian Fellowship Church, Strandtown, Belfast

**Michael Wardlow**
Chief Executive, Northern Ireland Council for Integrated Education

**Ethel White**
Agricultural Scientist, member of CRIS

# ECONI

## Publications

PATHWAYS
**For God and His Glory Alone**. A contribution relating some biblical principles to the situation in Northern Ireland. 2nd ed 1998 (£2.50)
**What Does the Lord Require of Us?** 1993 (£1)
**A Future with Hope.** Biblical Frameworks for Peace & Reconciliation in Northern Ireland. 2nd ed 1998 (£2.50)
**Beyond Fear, Suspicion and Hostility.** Evangelical - Roman Catholic relationships. A. Thomson, 1994 (£2)
**The Fractured Family.** Fundamentalists, Evangelicals and ECONI. A. Thomson, 1995 (£2)
**The Fire and the Hammer.** A Study of Jeremiah 6 - God's word to a complacent people. A. Thomson, 1997 (£2)
**The Politics of Holiness.** A. Thomson, 1998 (£2.50)

**Faith in Ulster.** Fifty contributors reflect on the question, 'What does For God and Ulster mean to you?' Edited A. Thomson, 1996 (£6)

**Great White Tent.** Nationalist reflections on Unionist identity. Edited by A. Thomson, Feb.1999 (£5)

**Action Packs** (£25 complete set)
Binder + 10 action packs on the following themes:
Peace; Forgiveness; Repentance; Truth; Reconciliation; Hope; Justice & Righteousness; Love; Citizenship; Servanthood

**Resource packs** - looseleaf - sermon notes/bible study material
£3.50
'Politics of Holiness - Separation & Sharing in a Divided Society'.
1997
'Jeremiah: a Prophet for our Time'. 1998
'A Time to Heal, The Church as a Community of Peace, Justice & Reconciliation'. 1998

**Enquiries to ECONI office:**
12 Wellington Place, BELFAST, BT1 6GE. Tel: 01232 325258
email admin@econi.org   web: http//www.econi.org